J 551.5
Lowery, Lawrence F.
How does the wind blow?

$10.95
ocn847763455
04/14/2014

How Does the Wind Blow?

WITHDRAWN

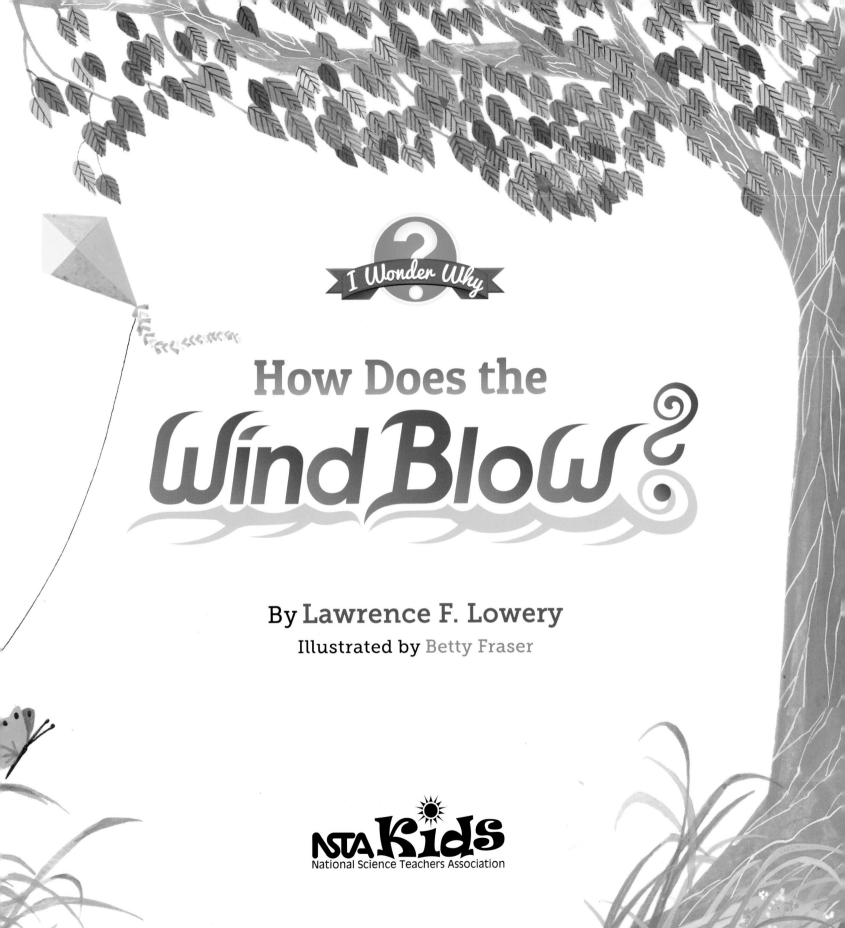

I Wonder Why

How Does the
Wind Blow?

By Lawrence F. Lowery

Illustrated by Betty Fraser

NSTA Kids
National Science Teachers Association

National Science Teachers Association

Claire Reinburg, Director
Jennifer Horak, Managing Editor
Andrew Cooke, Senior Editor
Amanda O'Brien, Associate Editor
Wendy Rubin, Associate Editor
Amy America, Book Acquisitions Coordinator

ART AND DESIGN
Will Thomas Jr., Director
Joseph Butera, Cover, Interior Design
Original illustrations by Betty Fraser

PRINTING AND PRODUCTION
Catherine Lorrain, Director

NATIONAL SCIENCE TEACHERS ASSOCIATION
David L. Evans, Executive Director
David Beacom, Publisher

1840 Wilson Blvd., Arlington, VA 22201
www.nsta.org/store
For customer service inquiries, please call 800-277-5300.

Copyright © 2013 by the National Science Teachers Association.
All rights reserved. Printed in the United States of America.
16 15 14 13   4 3 2 1

NSTA is committed to publishing material that promotes the best in inquiry-based science education. However, conditions of actual use may vary, and the safety procedures and practices described in this book are intended to serve only as a guide. Additional precautionary measures may be required. NSTA and the authors do not warrant or represent that the procedures and practices in this book meet any safety code or standard of federal, state, or local regulations. NSTA and the authors disclaim any liability for personal injury or damage to property arising out of or relating to the use of this book, including any of the recommendations, instructions, or materials contained therein.

PERMISSIONS
Book purchasers may photocopy, print, or e-mail up to five copies of an NSTA book chapter for personal use only; this does not include display or promotional use. Elementary, middle, and high school teachers may reproduce forms, sample documents, and single NSTA book chapters needed for classroom or noncommercial, professional-development use only. E-book buyers may download files to multiple personal devices but are prohibited from posting the files to third-party servers or websites, or from passing files to non-buyers. For additional permission to photocopy or use material electronically from this NSTA Press book, please contact the Copyright Clearance Center (CCC) (*www.copyright.com*; 978-750-8400). Please access *www.nsta.org/permissions* for further information about NSTA's rights and permissions policies.

Library of Congress Cataloging-in-Publication Data
Lowery, Lawrence F.
  How does the wind blow? / by Lawrence F. Lowery ; illustrated by Betty Fraser.
    pages cm. -- (I wonder why)
  Audience: K to grade 3.
  ISBN 978-1-938946-13-4 (print) -- ISBN 978-1-938946-71-4 (e-book) 1. Winds--Juvenile literature. I. Fraser, Betty, illustrator. II. Title.
  QC931.4.L68 2013
  551.51'8--dc23
                        2013020340

Cataloging-in-Publication Data are also available from the Library of Congress for the e-book.

Introduction

The *I Wonder Why* books are science books created specifically for young learners who are in their first years of school. The content for each book was chosen to be appropriate for youngsters who are beginning to construct knowledge of the world around them. These youngsters ask questions. They want to know about things. They are more curious than they will be when they are a decade older. Research shows that science is students' favorite subject when they enter school for the first time.

Science is both *what* we know and *how* we come to know it. What we know is the content knowledge that accumulates over time as scientists continue to explore the universe in which we live. How we come to know science is the set of thinking and reasoning processes we use to get answers to the questions and inquiries in which we are engaged.

Scientists learn by observing, comparing, and organizing the objects and ideas they are investigating. Children learn the same way. These thinking processes are among several inquiry behaviors that enable us to find out about our world and how it works. Observing, comparing, and organizing are fundamental to the more advanced thinking processes of relating, experimenting, and inferring.

The five books in this set of the *I Wonder Why* series focus on Earth science content. The materials of our Earth are mostly in the forms of solids (rocks and minerals), liquids (water), and gases (air). Inquiries about these materials are initiated by curiosity. When we don't know something about an area of interest, we try to understand it by asking questions and doing investigations. These five Earth science books are written from the learner's point of view: *How Does the Wind Blow?*; *Clouds, Rain, Clouds Again*; *Spenser and the Rocks*; *Environments of Our Earth*; and *Up, Up in a Balloon*. Children inquire about pebbles and rocks, rain and wind, and jungles and deserts. Their curiosity leads them to ask questions about land forms, weather, and climate.

The information in these books leads the characters and the reader to discover how wind can be measured and how powerful it can be, how the water cycle works, that living things need water to survive, and that plants and animals have adapted to different climate-related environments. They also learn how people have learned to fly in the ocean of air that surrounds Earth.

Each book uses a different approach to take the reader through simple scientific information. One book is expository, providing factual information. Several are narratives that allow a story to unfold. Another provides a historical perspective that tells how we gradually learn science through experimentations over time. The combination of different artwork, literary perspectives, and scientific knowledge brings the content to the reader through several instructional avenues.

In addition, the content in these books correlates to criteria set forth by national standards. Often the content is woven into each book so that its presence is subtle but powerful. The science activities in the Parent/Teacher Handbook section in each book enable learners to carry out their own investigations that relate to the content of the book. The materials needed for these activities are easily obtained, and the activities have been tested with youngsters to be sure they are age appropriate.

After students have completed a science activity, rereading or referring back to the book and talking about connections with the activity can be a deepening experience that stabilizes the learning as a long-term memory.

Air is almost everywhere.
It is all around you.
Cup your hands, and the air fills them.

Air is in all of our houses.
It is in all of the stores and ships.
Air is on top of the highest mountains.
It is down in the deepest caves.

Air is in you, too.

Air is almost everywhere,
but no one has ever seen it!

It has no color.
It has no smell.
You cannot taste it, even if you try.

Even so, you can learn about the air.
You can begin by watching things that are moved by air.

Air that moves is called wind.

Sometimes the wind's movement is slow.
Sometimes it blows fast.
Sometimes there is no wind at all.

When there is no wind, the smoke from chimneys
rises straight up toward the sky.
Leaves on trees do not move.
Papers stay where they are and do not fly about.
The air is very still.

On some days, you can feel the wind blowing softly against your face.
A light breeze is the name for air that moves slowly.

In a light breeze, leaves rustle with a soft sound.
Smoke drifts wherever the light breeze may take it.

There are times when the air moves a bit faster than a light breeze.

It moves fast enough to bend small twigs on trees and bushes.

It flutters the leaves on trees.

Air that moves objects like this is called a gentle breeze.

In a gentle breeze, small flags flutter and wave.

Have you ever felt a gentle breeze when you played in the open air?

Sometimes a wind is strong enough to blow small papers to and fro.
A wind that can do this is called a moderate wind.
A moderate wind blows a little bit harder than a gentle breeze.

In a moderate wind, small branches move this way and that.
They rub against each other, and you can hear them if you
stand nearby and listen.

Sometimes the wind blows so hard that small trees sway back and forth.
Leaves seem to whisper as they brush against one another.
A wind that blows this hard is called a fresh wind.

When a fresh wind blows across the water,
you can see curly white tops on the waves.
The white tops seem to dance on the water
in this kind of wind.

Sometimes air moves still more quickly than a fresh wind.

It shakes large branches of trees.

It blows off hats and makes your kite fly high.

No wonder a wind like this is called a strong wind!

A strong wind hums and sings as it blows
through telephone wires.
It makes the rain beat hard against windows.
It pulls at your umbrella and can turn it
inside out.

When a wind blows so hard that it makes
tall trees bend, the wind is called a gale.

A gale breaks off twigs.
It blows down signs.
It can break windows.

A gale can break large branches from a
tree. It can even blow down trees that
stand in its way.

Have you ever tried to walk against this kind of wind?
Walking can be hard on such a windy day.

A wind that is stronger than a gale is a dangerous wind.
It can blow the ocean into giant waves.

It can toss big boats onto the shore.

It can blow down street lights.

It can tear a building apart.

A wind that blows this strongly is called a hurricane.

A hurricane is a very, very strong wind. You must go someplace where you will be safe from this wind.

Don't watch the hurricane through a window because a hurricane can break windows and knock down trees.

There is another dangerous wind that is more powerful than a hurricane.
It is called a tornado.

You can hear the roar of this wind.
It sounds louder than a fleet of jets roaring by.
It is a wind that can lift houses and animals and trees into the air.
It can even lift a railroad car and smash it to the ground.

The air in a tornado spins like a top.
As it spins, it picks up dust and dirt that make it look very dark.

This dark, spinning tornado does not stay in one place very long.
It moves across the land. A tornado can do much damage before it
stops spinning.

Moving air can do many things.

It can rush about like an angry giant.

It can spin through towns like a giant top.

But most of the time, moving air is pleasant.

A light breeze can cool us on a hot summer day.

A moderate breeze can push our sailboats across a pond.

A fresh breeze will blow the autumn leaves from trees.

Although air cannot be seen, when it moves, you know it is there.

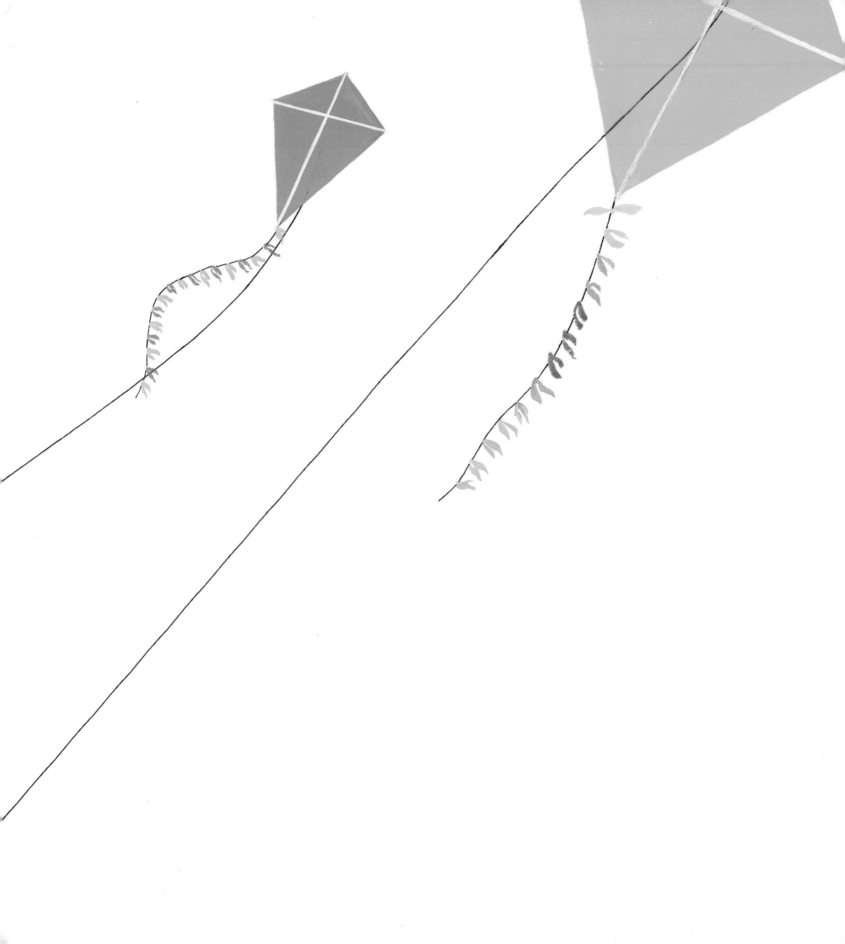